# Lisa Collins

# Activate your
# INNER POWER
# for a new life

EDITIONS VERGE-D'OR PUBLISHING

*Activate your INNER POWER for a new life*

By: Lisa Collins

Cover design: www.postermywall.com

Translation: www.deepl.com



©2024, Editions Verge-d'Or Publishing

ISBN: 978-2-924818-83-1

Editions Verge-d'Or Publishing

Mont Tremblant (Quebec) J8E 2S7 CANADA

E-mail address:

editionsvergedorpublishing@gmail.com

*To my family, with love,*

*Lisa*

# PROLOGUE

In an ever-changing world, where the pace of modern life seems to accelerate relentlessly, it's easy to get lost in the daily hustle and bustle. Expectations, responsibilities and distractions often pull us away from our deepest essence, from the inner strength that lies dormant within each of us. Yet at the heart of every individual lies an immeasurable power, a creative energy waiting to be awakened.

"Activate Your Inner Power for a New Life" is a journey, an invitation to explore the depths of your being and discover the limitless resources that reside there. This book is designed to guide you through 23 chapters, each revealing strategies, practices and reflections designed to help you reconnect to this vital force, learn to unleash your potential and transform your reality.

In these pages, you'll discover how to overcome the mental and emotional obstacles that stand in your way. You'll learn to cultivate mindfulness, develop your intuition and embrace your passions. This journey will lead you to an expanded state of consciousness, where every choice becomes a reflection of your true essence, and every action is guided by your inner power.

As you embark on this adventure, remember that change begins with you. By connecting to your inner power, you not only transform your own life, you also inspire those around you. Together, we can create a world where everyone lives in harmony with themselves and with others, a world where the inner power of each individual lights the way to a new life.

Open your heart and mind, and let yourself be carried away by this exploration. Your journey to discover your inner power begins here.

## WE ARE ONLY ENERGY

In the universe, everything is in perpetual motion. Stars shine, planets rotate around their axes, and even at the microscopic level, atoms dance in a complex symphony of forces and interactions. This ceaseless motion and dynamics is nothing other than a manifestation of a fundamenttal reality: we are all energy.

### The nature of energy

To understand this assertion, it's essential to define energy. In physics, energy is often described as the capacity to do work. It manifests itself in various forms: kinetic, potential, thermal, electrical, chemical, and many others. Each form of energy can be transformed into another, but energy never disappears. This principle of energy conservation is fundamental to our understanding of the world.

But beyond scientific definitions, energy is omnipresent in our daily lives. Every gesture, every thought, every emotion we experience is a form of energy. Our interactions with the world and with others are nothing less than energy exchanges. When we laugh, we share our positive energy; when we're angry, we give off darker energy. So our very existence is an energetic dance.

## The science behind our energetic nature

Modern science, particularly quantum physics, has revealed some fascinating truths about the nature of reality. At a subatomic level, matter itself is not as solid as it seems. Particles like electrons are both particles and waves, and their behavior can change depending on observation. This raises profound questions about consciousness and perception: if everything is energy, then our consciousness plays an active role in creating our reality.

Theories such as the Holographic Universe suggest that the reality we perceive is in fact a projection of the information contained on the surface of space. This means that every individual, every thought, every emotion contributes to the collective energy that shapes our experience. We are linked to a whole, an energetic carpet in which every thread has its importance.

## The impact of our emotions and thoughts

The concept that we are only energy is also echoed in Eastern philosophies and spiritual practices. Traditions such as Buddhism and Taoism teach that our thoughts and emotions create our reality. Meditation and mindfulness are practices that aim to harmonize our inner energy, making it brighter and connecting us to universal energy.

Scientific studies also show that our emotions can have a measurable impact on our physical health. Stress, for example, is a form of negative energy that can lead to illness. Conversely, positive emotions such as love and gratitude can strengthen our immune system and promote healing. This underlines the power of our inner energy and the importance of cultivating positive thoughts and emotions.

## The connection between all living beings

If we are all energy, this implies that we are all interconnected. Every living being emits a certain frequency of energy that can influence its environment and other living beings. Experiences of synchronicity, where events seem to occur in a meaningful and aligned way, can be interpreted as manifestations of this energetic connection.

In nature, this interconnection is visible in ecosystems where every element plays a vital role. Trees, animals, rivers and even rocks are constantly exchanging energy. In our modern society, this awareness of our energetic nature can be a powerful catalyst for change. By recognizing that we are all part of the same energetic fabric, we can act with greater compassion, respect and responsibility.

## Towards a new understanding of ourselves

Embracing the idea that we are only energy invites us to rethink our relationship with the world. It prompts us to question our choices, our behaviors and their impact on our environment and on others. It encourages us to seek a way of life that is in harmony with our energetic nature.

It's crucial to integrate this understanding into our education, health and relationships. By cultivating energetic awareness, we can create healthier, more resilient communities. By learning to manage our inner energy and connect with the energy of others, we can build a world where empathy and solidarity prevail.

We are all energy, a reality that transcends the boundaries of science and spirituality. By becoming aware of our energetic nature, we have the opportunity to transform our existence and that of our planet. By cultivating positive thoughts and emotions, connecting with others and respecting our environment, we can contribute to a future where the energy that unites us is a force for life, peace and harmony.

*"Spirituality doesn't mean being nice; it means being aware."*

— Anthony de Mello

(Free Translation)

BUT STILL?

**Energy bodies or subtle (non-physical) bodies**

There are several subtle bodies, of which the following seven are the most important:

1. Physical body (in relation to the first root chakra).

2. Etheric body (linked to the second chakra, the sacral chakra).

3. Emotional body (in relation to the third chakra, the solar plexus chakra).

4. Mental body (linked to the fourth chakra, the heart chakra).

5. Causal body or soul body (linked to the fifth chakra, the throat chakra).

6. Buddhist body or our higher consciousness (in relation to the sixth chakra, the third eye chakra).

7. Divine body (in relation to the seventh chakra, the coronal or crown chakra): synonymous with awareness of source, Love and unity.

Note that the different bodies are nested inside each other (like a Russian doll).

Humans have 7 major chakras or energy centers linked to the seven main energy bodies. Among other things, the chakras serve to balance and preserve the health of the energy bodies and aura. They cross the body at specific points, forwards and backwards.

The meridians also play a very important role.

For those who want to know more, there are some excellent, comprehensive books available on the market dedicated solely to energy bodies and their care, cleansing, treatment and healing.

*"Peace comes from within.*

*Don't look for it on the outside."*

— Buddha

(Free Translation)

# CARBON DNA AND CRYSTALLINE DNA: A JOURNEY TO THE HEART OF OUR INNER POWER

In the quest to understand our essence and inner power, it's essential to explore the mysteries of our DNA. This biological code, which holds the instructions for our development and functioning, goes far beyond simple biology. It represents a profound link between our body, mind and creative source.

## Carbon DNA: the thread of life

The DNA we know is made up of carbon molecules, which form the basis of life as we perceive it. Every cell in our bodies contains this precious genetic code, which influences not only our physical appearance, but also our behavior, emotions and even our spiritual potential. Scientists have discovered that our DNA reacts to the vibrations and energies that surround us. So our environment, thoughts and emotions can influence our DNA, opening the way to a deeper understanding of how we can shape our reality.

In the context of spirituality, carbon DNA can be seen as a channel through which we experience our humanity. Spiritual traditions often speak of the need to raise our vibratory frequency in order to harmonize our being. This can involve practices such as meditation, yoga and other forms of energy work that help us align our thoughts and emotions with our deeper essence.

### Crystalline DNA: a higher dimension

Alongside carbon DNA, many esoteric and spiritual traditions refer to the existence of crystalline DNA. This notion suggests the existence of a more evolved form of DNA, one that transcends the simple genetic code. Crystalline DNA is associated with higher consciousness, spiritual ascension and a state of being in which we are in perfect harmony with the universe.

This concept of crystalline DNA is based on the idea that, as we awaken spiritually and work on our personal development, we begin to activate latent aspects of our DNA. This can manifest as heightened intuition, psychic abilities and a deeper connection with our environment. Crystals, which are often used in energy therapy, are also seen as tools for activating this crystalline DNA, due to their own vibrational structures that can influence our energy field.

**The synergy between carbon and crystalline DNA**

True inner power emerges when we integrate these two aspects of our DNA. By recognizing the importance of our carbon DNA, we accept our humanity and the challenges that come with it. At the same time, by aspiring to activate our crystalline DNA, we open the door to infinite possibilities. This synergy enables us to live our full potential, integrate our authenticity and interact with the world in a more conscious way.

Exploring our DNA, at both the carbon and crystalline levels, invites us on an inner journey. It's a reminder that we are not just physical beings, but spiritual beings first and foremost, with a unique mission. By honoring and cultivating this synergy, we can awaken our inner power and contribute to the emergence of a higher consciousness.

In this chapter, we've scratched the surface of the depths of our DNA, illuminating its crucial role in our personal and spiritual development. By integrating the teachings of carbon DNA and crystalline DNA, we embark on a path of transformation that connects us to our purest essence. The search for inner power then becomes not only an individual journey, but also a step towards collective harmony, where each human being, as an extension of the universe, plays a vital role in the symphony of life.

*"What doesn't kill us makes us stronger."*

— Friedrich Nietzsche

(Free Translation)

## OUR DIVINE PLAN

In the vast panorama of human existence, the idea of a divine plan emerges like a common thread, a woven fabric of meaning and destiny. Each individual, each soul, is here to accomplish a unique mission, a work that often goes beyond our immediate comprehension. This chapter explores this profound concept, examining how the divine plan is articulated in our lives, and how we can access it to live in full harmony with our true essence.

### What is the divine plan?

The divine plan can be defined as a higher intention that guides our lives, directing us towards our ultimate goal. It's a spiritual journey that goes beyond mere material events. This plan is perceived as being linked to our soul, and is expressed through our aspirations, talents, challenges and life lessons. Every experience we have, whether joyful or painful, contributes to our evolution and the realization of this plan.

Many spiritual traditions teach that we choose our plan before we're born, selecting the challenges and circumstances that will help us grow. These choices, though sometimes difficult, are designed to propel us towards a deeper awakening and understanding of our true nature.

### Signs of the divine plan

So how can we recognize the signs of our divine plan in our daily lives? Often, they manifest themselves in the form of synchronicities, moments of intuition or meaningful encounters. These experiences may seem improbable, but they carry deep meaning. Coincidences that guide us towards new opportunities or unexpected encounters and change our perspective are indications that we are in tune with our plan.

Listening to our intuition is also crucial. This inner voice, often muffled by the noise of the world, speaks to us about our deepest desires and what resonates with our essence. When we take the time to connect with ourselves, we can better understand the paths open to us and make choices aligned with our divine plan.

## Challenges as growth opportunities

It's essential to understand that the challenges we face are not obstacles to our divine plan, but rather opportunities for growth. Every obstacle, every trial, is a lesson that prepares us to move forward on our path. Sometimes these challenges can seem overwhelming, but they are often catalysts for awakening. They push us to explore aspects of ourselves we might otherwise ignore, to develop our resilience and strengthen our connection with our spiritual essence.

By adopting this perspective, we can transform our relationship with difficulties. Instead of seeing them as failures or misfortunes, we can see them as necessary steps on our way to realizing our divine plan.

## Cultivating a connection with our divine plan

To live in alignment with our divine plan, it's essential to cultivate a regular practice of inner reflection and connection. This can take many forms: meditation, journaling, contemplation in nature, or even spiritual rituals. These moments of pause allow us to refocus, clarify our intentions and open up to the inspirations that emanate from our soul.

It's also beneficial to surround ourselves with people who share our vision and our spiritual quest. Enriching exchanges with like-minded souls can nourish our own path and remind us that we are not alone in this quest. Together, we can support each other as we move towards the realization of our respective plans.

### Living with intention and gratitude

Finally, living in accordance with our divine plan involves adopting an attitude of intention and gratitude. Every day, we have the opportunity to choose how we respond to the events of our lives. By cultivating an attitude of gratitude, we can recognize the small wonders and lessons that life offers us, even in the most difficult moments.

By committing ourselves to living in a conscious and aligned way, we open the door to an existence rich in meaning and fulfillment. Welcoming it with an open heart enables us to discover unsuspected dimensions of our being and our connection with the world.

Our divine plan is a journey, an exploration of ourselves and our place in the universe. By taking the time to connect with our essence, to recognize the signs, to transform our challenges into opportunities and to live with intention, we can discover the beauty and depth of this path that is offered to us. Every step we take on this path is a celebration of our existence, an affirmation of our inner power and a step towards a fully realized life.

*"Man is the reflection of his thoughts.*

*What he thinks, he becomes."*

— Mahatma Gandhi

(Free Translation)

## THE EARTH IS A SCHOOL

Every moment we live on this magnificent planet, a fascinating and complex place that offers us much more than breathtaking landscapes and abundant resources. The Earth, with its diversity of cultures, peoples and experiences, is in reality a school where every soul is invited to learn, grow and evolve. This chapter explores the idea that our existence on Earth is a learning opportunity, an educational adventure that prepares us for our true spiritual nature.

### Experiential learning

In this school called Earth, every experience we have is a valuable lesson. Joys, sorrows, successes and failures are all designed to help us understand human nature and develop our consciousness. Every relationship we form, every challenge we overcome, and every moment of contemplation is an opportunity for personal growth.

We come here with a baggage of experiences and lessons to integrate, but it's essential to understand that true wisdom doesn't lie solely in the accumulation of theoretical knowledge. It's by living each moment to the full, being present to our emotions and open to the lessons life has to offer, that we can truly learn. Earth teaches us through a variety of situations, challenging us to develop our empathy, resilience and capacity to love.

## Challenges as learning catalysts

Life on Earth isn't always easy. Challenges and trials are an integral part of our journey. They are often perceived as obstacles, but in reality they are catalysts for learning. Every trial we encounter is an opportunity to question our beliefs, our motivations and our ability to bounce back.

When we face difficult situations, we are invited to explore aspects of ourselves we might never have discovered otherwise. These moments of crisis push us to step out of our comfort zone and develop essential skills such as patience, compasssion and wisdom. In this way, challenges become teachers, preparing us for a richer, more fulfilling life.

## The diversity of human experience

The beauty of our earthly school also lies in the diversity of human experience. Every culture, every tradition, every story is a piece of humanity's vast puzzle. By interacting with people from different backgrounds, we have the opportunity to learn from a variety of perspectives and enrich our understanding of the world.

Travelling, whether physically or through the exchange of ideas, enables us to step outside our own frame of reference and discover ways of life, beliefs and values that are foreign to us. This open-mindedness is essential to our personal and collective development. By embracing this diversity, we cultivate our capacity to be citizens of the world, aware of and respectful of the differences that surround us.

## The teachers

In this school called Earth, there are teachers who guide us on our journey. These teachers can take many forms: mentors, friends, books, even nature itself. Every encounter, every interaction, every moment of silence in nature can teach us valuable lessons.

Nature, in particular, is an invaluable teacher. She teaches us about harmony, the cycle of life and the need to preserve our environment. By reconnecting with her, we can learn profound lessons about patience, resilience and respect for the interconnections that exist in our ecosystem.

## The quest for self and spiritual awakening

Ultimately, Earth is a school that prepares us for a quest for self and spiritual awakening. Every lesson we learn, every challenge we overcome, brings us closer to our true essence. As we grow, we develop a deeper awareness of our place in the universe and our connection with everything around us.

This quest for self leads us to question our personal mission, what we wish to achieve during our time on this planet. It invites us to explore our passions, talents and potential, inspiring us to live an authentic and meaningful life.

Earth is much more than just a place to live; it's a school where every moment is an opportunity to learn and grow. By integrating the lessons life has to offer, celebrating the diversity of human experience and listening to the teachers around us, we can embark on a path of personal and spiritual fulfillment. Ultimately, our time on this planet is an adventure that prepares us for a richer, more conscious and harmonious existence. It is in this school that we discover our potential and awaken to our true essence.

*"Spiritual life does not withdraw from the world*

*world*

*but lies deep within it.*

— Thomas Merton

(Free Translation)

# EVERYTHING IS ALREADY WITHIN US

In the hustle and bustle of modern life, we often tend to look outside ourselves for answers, solutions and resources. We chase after validations, successes and possessions, hoping they'll fill an inner void. Yet the fundamental truth we need to integrate is this: everything is already within us. This chapter explores the inner power that lies dormant within each of us, and how we can recognize, cultivate and express it in our daily lives.

## Recognizing our innate potential

Each of us is endowed with unlimited potential. At birth, we come into the world with a pure essence, a unique set of talents, passions and dreams. Over the years, however, we learn to conform to the expectations of others, adapt to societal norms and often lose sight of our authenticity. This disconnect can create a sense of dissatisfaction, self-doubt and a perpetual search for something external.

Recognizing that everything is already within us requires an act of courage and vulnerability. It involves looking in the mirror and asking deep questions: Who am I really? What are my deepest passions? What values define me? This process of introspection is essential to reconnect with our inner power.

## The importance of self-acceptance

One of the keys to accessing our inner power is self-acceptance. Too often, we judge and criticize our imperfections, compare ourselves to others and focus on our weaknesses. However, every aspect of ourselves, even those we perceive as flaws, is part of our uniqueness.

Accepting who we are, with our strengths and weaknesses, is a liberating act. It frees us from the shackles of judgment and shame, and allows us to embrace our true essence. By cultivating self-acceptance, we begin to unleash our potential and realize that the answers we seek externally already reside within us.

## Cultivating self-confidence

Self-confidence is one of the pillars of inner power. It develops when we recognize our abilities, celebrate our successes, even the smallest ones, and face up to our fears. Every time we step out of our comfort zone and dare to take risks, we strengthen our self-confidence.

It's also crucial to remember that confidence doesn't mean the absence of doubt. On the contrary, it means moving forward despite those doubts, believing in our abilities even when circumstances seem unfavorable. By cultivating this confidence, we open ourselves up to new possibilities and a more authentic life.

## The power of intuition

Our intuition is another manifestation of our inner power. It's often described as an inner voice, an instinct or a gut feeling that guides us in our choices. However, in the chaos of everyday life, it's easy to ignore it, repress it or confuse it with our fears.

To reconnect with our intuition, it's important to practice inner listening. This can be done through moments of silence, meditation or writing. By taking the time to sit and listen, we can access the inner wisdom that knows what's right for us. Intuition then becomes a beacon, a guide that helps us navigate through life's uncertainties.

### Inspired action

Recognizing that everything is already within us doesn't mean we have to stand still. On the contrary, it inspires us to act. Inspired action is that which flows from our deepest essence, our passions and our dreams. It's when we act in alignment with our inner truth that we experience true fulfillment.

It's important to remember that every little action counts. Whether sharing a talent, pursuing a passion or helping others, every gesture is an affirmation of our inner power. By taking action, we create waves of change not only in our own lives, but also in the lives of others.

### Awakening our community

When we reconnect to our inner power, we also have the ability to inspire and uplift those around us. By sharing our story, our learnings and our authenticity, we create a space where others can also feel safe to explore their own power.

Awakening our inner community means supporting others on their journey, celebrating their successes and encouraging them to embrace their own essence. Together, we form a network of light, where everyone contributes to the collective strength.

Everything is already within us. This statement, though simple, is incredibly powerful. By reconnecting to our essence, cultivating self-acceptance, self-confidence and listening to our intuition, we can unleash our unlimited potential. Far from looking outside ourselves for answers, we must delve deep within ourselves to discover the richness that lies within. By acting with inspiration and uplifting our community, we help create a world where everyone can shine in their full power. The key is there, within us, ready to be used.

*"Meditation brings wisdom;*

*lack of meditation leaves ignorance.*

*Know what guides you*

*and what holds you back."*

— Buddha

(Free Translation)

## REMEMBER WHO YOU ARE

In life's complex journey, it's easy to get lost in the expectations, roles and identities we adopt. We often get caught up in the demands of society, the opinions of others, and the pressures of our daily lives. Yet deep within us, a gentle, persistent voice reminds us of our true essence. This chapter explores the importance of remembering who we are, and how reconnecting with our inner power can transform our lives.

### The quest for our authentic identity

From an early age, we are conditioned by external influences: our families, our friends, our upbringing, and the culture in which we live. These influences shape our perception of ourselves, encouraging us to adopt behaviors and beliefs that don't always reflect our true essence. Over time, we can find ourselves playing roles that don't resonate with our heart, losing sight of who we really are.

The first step to remembering who you are is to engage in a process of introspection. Taking the time to reflect on our deepest values, passions and authentic desires is essential. What makes us tick? What activities bring us true happiness? By answering these questions, we begin to unearth the layers of condi-tioning and reconnect with our authentic identity.

### The importance of self-reflection

Self-reflection is a powerful tool for reconnecting with our essence. It can take many forms: journaling, meditation, or simply spending time in solitude. In these quiet moments, we have the opportunity to listen to our inner voice, look within ourselves and identify the thoughts and beliefs that serve or hinder us.

It's also useful to ask yourself some provocative questions: What are my fears? What limiting beliefs have I adopted? By exploring these aspects of ourselves, we can begin to understand the patterns that hold us back and challenge them. Self-reflection allows us to clear the path towards a deeper understanding of who we really are.

## Free yourself from external expectations

One of the main obstacles to reconnecting with our true essence lies in the expectations we have of others. Whether it's the pressure to succeed, to conform to social norms, or to meet family expectations, these influences can distance us from our authenticity. Remembering who we are involves freeing ourselves from these expectations and making choices that resonate with our heart.

It takes courage. It can be difficult to disappoint those around us, but it's crucial to remember that living an authentic life is an act of self-respect. When we choose to act in accordance with our essence, we send a powerful message to those around us: the importance of authenticity.

## The power of intuition

Our intuition, often described as an inner compass, plays a key role in the process of reconnecting with our essence. It guides us, enlightens us and helps us make choices in line with our true nature. However, in the noise and stress of everyday life, it's easy to ignore this voice.

To cultivate our intuition, it's essential to create moments of silence and tranquility. This can be achieved through meditation, walking in nature or simply taking the time to breathe deeply. By opening up to our intuition, we can discover profound truths about ourselves and our life path.

## Celebrating our uniqueness

Remembering who we are also means celebrating our uniqueness. Each individual is a unique blend of experiences, talents and perspectives. By recognizing the value we bring to the world, we can begin to embrace our authenticity and express ourselves without reserve.

This celebration of self can manifest itself in many ways: by sharing our talents, pursuing our passions, or engaging in activities that inspire us. By living our authenticity to the full, we positively influence our environment and encourage others to do the same.

## Community impact

Finally, remembering who we are can be facilitated by the support of a caring community. Surrounded by people who encourage us to be ourselves, we are better able to free ourselves from judgment and comparison. A community that celebrates authenticity allows us to grow and flourish in our true essence.

Participating in support groups, workshops or sharing circles can provide a safe space to explore our identity and aspirations. These exchanges nourish our self-confidence and strengthen our sense of belonging.

Remembering who we are is an ongoing journey, a process of self-discovery and re-evaluation. By engaging in self-reflection, freeing ourselves from external expectations, listening to our intuition and celebrating our uniqueness, we can reconnect to our inner power. This reconnection enables us to live a more authentic, fulfilling life aligned with our essence. In this quest, we discover

not only who we are, but also the beauty and
potential we bring to the world.

*"Quality of life does not depend

external circumstances,

but of the inner state."*

— Epictetus

(Free Translation)

In the universe around us, everything is energy. Every thought, every emotion, every living being vibrates at a unique frequency. Understanding frequencies and dimensions is important for accessing our inner power and successfully navigating the many layers of reality. This chapter examines how these concepts interact and how they can help us realize our full potential.

## The vibratory nature of existence

Everything that exists, from atoms to galaxies, is made up of vibrating energy. We saw this earlier in the book. Quantum physics teaches us that even the most solid matter is, in reality, a form of energy that oscillates at specific frequencies. These vibrations influence not only our environment, but also our inner state.

When we become aware of our own vibratory frequency, we discover that our thoughts and emotions play a central role in modulating this frequency. Positive thoughts, for example, raise our vibration, while negative emotions lower it. By learning to cultivate higher thoughts and emotions, we can adjust our personal frequency and, consequently, our experience of life.

## Emotional frequencies

Emotions are powerful vibratory manifestations. Each emotion has a distinct frequency that influences our well-being and our perception of reality. Emotions such as joy, love and gratitude vibrate at high frequencies, while emotions such as fear, anger and sadness vibrate at lower frequencies.

Recognizing and understanding these emotional frequencies is crucial to accessing our inner power. By cultivating positive emotions, we create an environment that fosters enriching experiences aligned with our true essence, our original being. This can be achieved through practices such as meditation, gratitude or visualization, which raise our vibratory state and connect us to our inner potential.

**Dimensions of reality**

The notion of dimensions goes beyond simple spatial measurement. In a spiritual context, dimensions represent different levels of consciousness and experience. Each dimension is characterized by a specific vibratory frequency, and our state of being determines which dimension we access.

We live mainly in the third dimension, where we experience separation, linear time, conflict and physical limitations. However, there are other dimensions, such as the fourth dimension, often associated with consciousness and time, the fifth dimension, which is linked to unconditional love, unity and co-creation, and other even higher dimensions.

By becoming aware of these dimensions, we can begin to transcend our current reality and access higher states of consciousness. This requires inner work, raising our vibratory frequency and opening up to wider perspectives.

**The importance of alignment**

To navigate effectively between these

frequencies and dimensions, it's essential to maintain a state of alignment. Alignment occurs when our thoughts, emotions and actions are in harmony with our true essence. This state of being enables us to access higher dimensions and manifest our inner power.

To cultivate this alignment, it's important to develop a daily practice that helps us stay centered and aware. This can include meditation, yoga, gratitude rituals, or any other practice that resonates with us. By investing time in nurturing our mind and body, we create a space for our vibrational frequency to flourish.

### Connecting with the universe

Once we are aware of our frequency and state of alignment, we can begin to connect more deeply with the universe. This connection reminds us that we are not separate from the whole, but rather integrated into a vast network of energy and consciousness.

Awareness of this interconnectedness allows us to understand that our actions and thoughts have repercussions not only on our own lives, but also on those of others and on the universe as a whole. By choosing to vibrate at higher frequencies, we contribute to raising collective energy and creating a more harmonious world.

### Co-creating our reality

Understanding frequencies and dimensions also offers us the possibility of co-creating our reality. By being aware of our inner power, we can use our thoughts, emotions and intentions to shape our life experience. This means taking responsibility for what we create and acting with intention.

The Law of Attraction, which states that we attract what we vibrate, plays a crucial role in this process. By cultivating positive thoughts and emotions, we send clear signals to the universe, attracting experiences and opportunities that match our vibratory frequency and feelings.

Frequencies and dimensions are fundamental concepts for understanding our existence and inner power. By becoming aware of our own vibratory frequency, cultivating positive emotions and aligning ourselves with our essence, our original being, we can navigate between dimensions of reality and access higher states of consciousness. Remembering that everything is interconnected allows us to co-create our reality and elevate not only our own experience, but also that of the world around us. By embracing our inner power, we become agents of change, capable of transforming our lives and inspiring others.

*"What is past has fled, what you hope for is absent, but the present is yours."*

— Arabic proverb

(Free Translation)

**EVERYONE IS LOOKING FOR EACH OTHER**

In the hustle and bustle of modern life, it's easy to feel lost, as if we're all searching for a meaning, a direction, a personal truth. This sense of searching is universal, transcending age, culture and circumstance. This chapter explores this common human quest, how it manifests itself, and how it is intrinsically linked to our inner power.

**The quest for self: a universal human experience**

Since the dawn of time, human beings have questioned their very existence. Who am I? What is my purpose? Why am I here? These fundamental questions are at the heart of the human experience. Every individual, at one time or another, is faced with these existential questions, whether in moments of joy or in times of crisis.

This quest for self is often triggered by significant events: the loss of a loved one, a break-up, a career change, or even simple dissatisfaction with our current life. These moments of self-questioning push us to delve deep within ourselves and search for answers that elude us. Understanding that everyone is searching for themselves can bring a sense of solidarity and understanding to our own struggles.

### The different types of search

The search for self can take many forms. For some, it may involve physical travel, discovering new horizons and different cultures. For others, it takes the form of inner exploration, through meditation, therapy or spiritual practices. Each path is unique, but all share a common goal: to rediscover meaning and connection to oneself.

In today's society, access to information and resources is unprecedented. Books, podcasts and personal development workshops abound, offering tools for navigating this quest. However, it's essential to remember that, despite the abundance of resources, true self-knowledge comes from within. The answers we seek are often buried beneath layers of conditioning, patterns and limiting beliefs.

## Obstacles to self-discovery

Although the quest for self is natural, it is not without obstacles. Fears, doubts and the expectations of others can get in the way. Fear of the unknown can paralyze us and prevent us from making bold decisions. What's more, comparisons with others can reinforce our sense of insecurity and distance us from our own truth.

It's crucial to recognize these obstacles and confront them. This requires courage and a willingness to explore the parts of ourselves we may have ignored or repressed. By engaging in this process, we can begin to free ourselves from the chains that prevent us from accessing our inner power.

## The importance of authenticity

At the heart of the quest for self lies the search for authenticity. Being authentic means recognizing who we really are, without artifice or mask. It means accepting our strengths and weaknesses, recognizing our passions and acting in accordance with our values.

Authenticity is a source of inner power. When we live in alignment with our true essence, we feel more at peace, more confident and more fulfilled. It also enables us to attract relationships and experiences that resonate with our authentic vibration, creating a virtuous circle of fulfillment.

## The wisdom of hardship

On our journey, it's important to remember that trials, though often painful, are also powerful teachers. Every challenge we encounter offers us an opportunity for learning and growth. Moments of suffering can prompt us to question our choices, our beliefs and our identity.

By facing our trials with openness and curiosity, we can learn valuable lessons and strengthen our resilience. This process of transformation can bring us closer to our inner power, enabling us to rise above our circumstances and discover aspects of ourselves we'd never have suspected.

## Connecting with others in the search for self

The quest for self is not an isolated journey.

In fact, connecting with others can enrich our understanding of ourselves. Sharing our experiences, listening to other people's stories and engaging in deep discussion allows us to broaden our perspective and discover facets of ourselves that we might not have explored on our own.

Community plays a crucial role in this quest. Whether through support groups, sharing circles or genuine friendships, human connections remind us that we are not alone in our search. Together, we can support each other, celebrate our victories and learn from our failures.

### Awakening to our inner power

Ultimately, everyone's searching for themselves, because we're all in search of our inner power, our divinity. This path to self-discovery is an invitation to reconnect with our essence, our creativity and our unlimited potential. By taking the time to get to know ourselves, to accept our imperfections and to act with authenticity, we can unleash our true power and live a life full of meaning.

This quest is a never-ending journey, a process of awakening that continues throughout our existence. At every step, we discover new truths about ourselves and our place in the world. In making this search, we take a step towards a richer, more fulfilling life, more connected to our inner power.

Everyone is searching, and this search is an expression of our humanity. By recognizing that we are not alone in our journey, we can engage with compassion and curiosity in our own exploration. Through introspection, authenticity and connection with others, we have the opportunity to discover our inner power and live a life that resonates with our true essence. The search for self is a sacred path, and every step we take brings us a little closer to realizing our potential.

*"The best wealth is that of the soul."*

— Socrates

(Free Translation)

# ILLUSION: HOW TO GET OUT OF IT

External influences shape our thoughts, behaviors and choices, and it becomes essential to ask ourselves a fundamental question: are we really in control of our lives, or are we trapped in a matrix of conditioning and limiting beliefs? This chapter examines ways of breaking out of this matrix, regaining our autonomy and living in alignment with our true essence.

## Understanding the matrix

The matrix is often seen as a set of social, cultural and psychological structures that condition us to think and act in a certain way. It manifests itself in social norms, family expectations, religious beliefs and political ideologies. As we grow up, we integrate these influences without always questioning them, which can lead us to live a life that doesn't really belong to us.

To break out of this matrix, it's essential to become aware of its existence. This starts with careful observation of our environment and our own thoughts. What beliefs do we take for granted? What voices influence us? And so on. By identifying these elements, we can begin to understand the mechanisms that keep us trapped.

## The need for introspection

Introspection is an effective tool for exploring our inner selves and understanding the motivations that guide our actions. In a world saturated with distractions, it's important to take the time to settle down and listen to our inner voice. This can be done through practices such as meditation, journaling or simply by spending time alone with ourselves.

By asking ourselves deep questions about our desires, values and aspirations, we can begin to uncover the truths hidden beneath layers of conditioning. What makes us truly happy? What passions have we neglected? This introspection helps us to reconnect with our essence and identify aspects of our lives that need changing.

## Challenging limiting beliefs

Once we're aware of our conditioning, it's time to challenge the limiting beliefs that hold us back. These beliefs, often unconscious, influence our perception of ourselves and our potential. For example, thoughts such as "I'm not good enough" or "I don't deserve success" can prevent us from acting in accordance with our true nature.

To deconstruct these beliefs, we must first identify and analyze them. Where do they come from? Are they based on real facts or misperceptions? By questioning them, we can begin to replace these negative thoughts with positive affirmations and supportive beliefs. This mental transformation is an essential step towards our emancipation.

## Raising our vibratory frequency

Breaking out of the artificial matrix also means raising our vibratory frequency. As mentioned earlier in this book, our emotional and mental state affects our vibration. By cultivating positive emotions such as gratitu-de, love and joy, we can move away from the negative energies that keep us trapped.

Practices such as meditation, yoga and mindfulness can help raise our frequency. Spending time in nature, practicing creative activities or surrounding ourselves with inspiring people are also effective ways of nourishing our mind and heart. A high vibratory state enables us to connect to higher dimensions of consciousness and move away from the limiting influences of the matrix.

## Making conscious decisions

To break out of the artificial matrix, it's crucial to make decisions with full awareness. This means acting with intention, rather than reacting automatically to external stimuli. Every choice we make, whether it's about our career, our relationships or our hobbies, must be in line with our true essence.

When we make conscious decisions, we commit ourselves to living in harmony with our values and aspirations. This may mean making difficult choices, such as leaving toxic relationships or quitting a job that no longer satisfies us. However, each step towards a more authentic life strengthens our personal power and our connection to our true selves.

## Connect to our support community

Breaking out of the matrix is not a journey we have to undertake alone. Finding a supportive community of like-minded people can help. These connections remind us that we are not alone in our quest for truth and authenticity.

Participating in discussion groups, workshops or spiritual retreats can offer us a space to share our experiences and learn from others. These exchanges nourish our personal growth and strengthen our determination to live in harmony with our essence.

## The practice of gratitude and acceptance

Finally, to break out of the matrix and raise our vibrational frequencies, it's important to cultivate a practice of gratitude and acceptance. Acknowledging the lessons each experience brings us, even the most difficult ones, helps us to free ourselves from victimization and other patterns. By accepting our journey and expressing gratitude for the challenges we've overcome, we strengthen our resilience and personal power.

This positive attitude enables us to see opportunities in obstacles and transform our perception of life. By cultivating gratitude, we create space for abundance and joy, which helps us move away from the limitations of the matrix.

To sum up this chapter, stepping out of the matrix is a journey of self-discovery, challenging limiting beliefs and patterns, and connecting with our inner power. By practicing introspection, raising our vibrational frequency, making conscious decisions and surrounding ourselves with a supportive community, we can free ourselves from the chains that hold us back. This process requires courage and commitment, but it opens the way to an authentic life, rich in meaning and fulfillment.

Freedom is at hand, and it begins with a choice: to live in accordance with our true being.

*"We are what we think. Everything we are emerges with our thoughts. With our thoughts, we make the world."*

— Buddha

(Free Translation)

## MAKING ROOM FOR SOUL AND LIGHT

In an often tumultuous world, where noise and stress seem to dominate our daily lives, it becomes crucial to take a break, slow down the pace and reconnect with our deepest essence. This chapter is dedicated to the idea that true inner strength can only emerge when we make room for our soul and the light.

### The quest for inner space

The first step in welcoming our soul is to create an inner space conducive to reflection and introspection. This requires recognizing and releasing the emotional and mental burdens that hinder us. Taking the time to meditate, write in a journal or simply sit in silence can allow our minds to calm down. This process of clearing is essential; it enables us to distinguish our inner voice from external distractions.

### The voice of the soul

Once we've made space, we begin to hear the voice of our soul, that part of us that knows what's really important. It doesn't always manifest itself forcefully; often it comes in the form of a gentle intuition or a slight impulse. Listening to this voice takes practice and a willingness to be vulnerable. It may involve asking questions that are sometimes difficult to answer, and exploring our deepest fears and desires.

### The inner light

Once we've opened this space, our inner light can begin to shine more brightly. This light represents our potential, our creativity and our spiritual connection. It is nourished by our passions, our dreams and our desire to evolve. By taking the time to cultivate this light, we learn to align ourselves with our true selves, enabling us to live authentically and meaningfully.

### The importance of gratitude

To make room for this light, gratitude plays a fundamental role. Acknowledging the small and large blessings in our lives helps us to raise our vibratory frequency. Gratitude transforms our perception, enabling us to see the beauty in the details, even in difficult moments. By integrating a regular practice of gratitude into our daily lives, we pave the way for more love and light in our lives.

### Freeing yourself from limiting beliefs

For our soul to flourish, it's also essential to free ourselves from limiting beliefs and negative thought patterns. These barriers, often inherited from our past or society, can obscure our inner light. By becoming aware of these beliefs, we can challenge them and choose to transform them. This process of liberation is an act of courage and determination.

### Raising our vibration

As we make room for our soul and nurture our light, our personal vibration rises. This upliftment has an impact not only on our own lives, but also on our environment and the people around us. By radiating our light, we have the power to inspire and uplift others, creating a chain of positivity and transformation.

Making room for soul and light is an ongoing self-exploration that requires patience and commitment. By becoming aware of our inner power, we can not only transform our own existence, but also contribute to a brighter, more harmonious world. Every step we take in this direction brings us closer to our true essence, enabling us to live fully and embrace life with gratitude and Love. On this journey, we discover that the light that shines within us is an inexhaustible source of strength and inspiration, ready to illuminate our path and that of others.

*"Darkness cannot drive out darkness; only light can. Hate cannot drive out hate; only love can."*

— Martin Luther King Jr.

(Free Translation)

# FREQUENCY ELEVATION, ACTIVATION AND INTEGRATION

In the quest for inner power and spirituality, the idea of raising frequencies emerges as a fundamental concept. This chapter explores how we can raise our vibratory frequency, activate our hidden potential, and integrate and embody these transformations in our daily lives.

## Understanding vibratory frequencies

Everything in the universe vibrates at a certain frequency, including our thoughts, emotions and bodies. Higher frequencies are often associated with states of Love, joy, peace and creativity, while lower frequencies can be linked to fear, anger or sadness. Becoming aware of our own vibratory frequency is crucial to navigating the path of spiritual growth.

## Raising our frequency

Raising our frequency starts with awareness. What thoughts and emotions are holding us back? What habits or environmental influences are dragging us down? By identifying these elements, we can begin to make conscious choices to raise our vibration.

Practices such as meditation, yoga and mindfulness are effective tools for raising our frequency. By focusing on our breathing and cultivating a state of presence, we can release tension and open the way to higher energies. What's more, spending time in nature, listening to inspiring music or practicing gratitude are all ways of raising our vibration.

## Activating our potential

Once we've begun to raise our frequency, we enter the activa-tion phase. This is when we discover the talents and abilities that were latent within us. This activation can manifest itself in many different ways: in overflowing creativity, increased mental clarity, or even stronger intuition.

To activate our full potential, it's important to

give ourselves permission to explore and experiment. This may mean stepping out of our comfort zone, trying new activities or learning new skills. Each new trial brings us a little closer to our authentic essence, and enables us to discover aspects of ourselves we didn't know we had.

## Integrating transformations

Integration is where all these new energies and discoveries take root and become incarnated in our daily lives. This is where we learn to live in harmony with our higher frequency. This may require adjustments in our relationships, work and lifestyle.

Integration also requires patience and self-compassion. Transformations don't always happen in a linear fashion, and challenges can arise. However, every obstacle is an opportunity for learning and growth. By staying grounded in our practice and cultivating an open attitude, we can move gracefully through these periods.

## Balance and harmony

As we integrate these changes, it becomes essential to seek balance. Raising our frequency and activating our potential doesn't mean neglecting the darker aspects of our personality or experience. Accepting our humanity, including our fears and doubts, is an essential part of the journey. Harmony lies in accepting all our facets, and that's where we find true inner power.

Frequency elevation, activation and integration are interconnected processes that guide us on the path of self-discovery and spirituality. By taking the time to work on our vibratory frequency, activate our potential and integrate these transformations, we open ourselves up to a richer, more fulfilling life. On this journey, we realize that inner power lies not only in what we accomplish, but also in our capacity to love, learn and grow. As we ascend, we become beacons of light, inspiring those around us to do the same.

*"We are not human beings having a spiritual experience; we are spiritual beings having a human experience."*

—Pierre Teilhard de Chardin

(Free Translation)

## CLEANING, PURIFICATION

In our journey towards inner power and spirituality, cleansing and purification emerge as essential steps. This chapter discusses the importance of releasing stagnant energies, getting rid of toxic thoughts and emotions, and creating a sacred space to welcome light and growth.

### The importance of energetic cleansing

Just as a physical space can accumulate dust and clutter, our minds and bodies can be invaded by negative energies. These energies can come from a variety of sources: toxic relationships, unresolved past experiences, or even the influence of the media and our environment. Energy cleansing involves identifying these sources of burden and releasing them to allow our true essence to shine through.

## Cleaning practices

There are many practices we can adopt to achieve this cleansing. Meditation is one of the most powerful. By sitting quietly and focusing our mind, we can observe our thoughts without judgment. This observation enables us to become aware of recurring patterns that no longer serve us, and to let them go.

Purification rituals, such as fumigation with sage or incense, are also effective. Smoke is often used to cleanse negative energies from a space or person. By creating a sacred environment, we establish a deeper connection with our spirituality.

## Purification of body and mind

Purification isn't just about energy; it also extends to our bodies and minds. Adopting a conscious diet, rich in fresh, natural foods, helps to eliminate physical toxins. Hydration is just as crucial, as water purifies and revitalizes our cells.

On a mental level, it's important to practice gratitude and positivity. Cultivating benevolent, optimistic thoughts is an act of mental purification. It helps us create a peaceful inner environment, conducive to spirituality.

### Emotional release

Cleansing and purification also involve releasing repressed emotions. We often carry within us old wounds that can create energetic blockages. Taking the time to cry, express our anger or share our fears with people we trust contributes to this process of liberation. Therapy, sharing circles or even writing can be invaluable tools for working through and purging these emotions.

### Creating a sacred space

Once we've cleaned up, it's essential to create a sacred space that reflects our new state of being. This can be done by creating a meditation corner, adding crystals, candles or objects that resonate with our essence. This space becomes a sanctuary where we can reconnect with our soul and our spirituality.

### Renewal energy

Cleansing and purification open the door to an energy of renewal. When we rid ourselves of the old, we make way for the new. This can manifest itself in unexpected opportunities, new relationships, or flourishing creativity. Welcoming this renewal with an open mind enables us to align ourselves more closely with our spiritual path.

To sum up this chapter, cleansing and purification are necessary practices for anyone who aspires to discover their inner power. By freeing ourselves from emotional burdens, stagnant energies and negative thoughts, we create a space conducive to growth, healing and spiritual fulfillment. Through these processes, we learn to honor ourselves and reconnect to our divine essence. Ultimately, the journey of cleansing and purification becomes a celebration of life, an invitation to love our light and live our truth to the full.

*"Your task is not to look for love, but simply to look for and find all the barriers within you that you've built up against it."*

— Rumi

(Free Translation)

## DEPROGRAMMING AND REPROGRAMMING

The quest for inner power often begins with awareness. We are all influenced by our environment, upbringing and collective beliefs. These influences shape our perception of ourselves and the world around us. However, to access our true potential, we need to undertake a process of deprogramming and reprogramming.

### Deprogramming: releasing limiting beliefs

Deprogramming is the process by which we identify and deconstruct the beliefs that limit us. These beliefs can be deeply rooted in us from childhood and even before, often inherited from our parents, ancestors, upbringing or culture. They manifest themselves as negative thoughts, fears or self-destructive behaviors.

To begin this process, we need to become aware of these beliefs. Practices such as meditation, journaling or therapy can help bring these patterns to light. Once identified, they can be challenged. Why do we believe we're not good enough? Where does this fear of failure come from? By exploring these questions, we can begin to unravel the fabric of our conditioning.

### Reprogramming: building new beliefs

Reprogramming is the next step, where we replace limiting beliefs with positive affirmations and constructive thoughts. This requires a clear intention and a commitment to nourish our minds with ideas that support our growth.

Visualization techniques, affirmations and repetition are powerful tools for this reprogramming. For example, by repeating daily affirmations such as "I am capable", "I deserve success" or "I am at peace with myself", we begin to reshape our inner dialogue.

Reprogramming is not limited to thoughts. It also extends to our actions. By acting on our new beliefs, we reinforce our new identity. This may involve stepping out of our comfort zone, facing our fears and engaging in activities that nourish our soul.

## Integration: alignment with our essence

Deprogramming and reprogramming are not isolated processes, but rather steps in a larger journey towards alignment with our true essence. This journey requires patience and perseverance. Old beliefs can resurface, and it's essential to approach them with compassion and understanding.

As we integrate these new beliefs into our daily lives, we begin to feel a transformation. Renewed self-confidence, clarity of mind and a deep connection with our inner self emerge. This process enables us to access our inner power, live with authenticity and manifest our deepest desires.

Deprogramming and reprogramming are essential tools for anyone who aspires to harness their inner power. By freeing our minds from the shackles of the past and cultivating uplifting beliefs, we open the door to unlimited potential. This journey, though sometimes difficult, is an adventure in self-discovery, an exploration of the depths of our being that leads us to a life full of meaning, joy and spiritual fulfillment.

*"My strength is my gentleness."*

— Sandrine Fillassier

(Free Translation)

EXPANDED AWARENESS

Expanding consciousness is a central concept in the quest for inner power and spirituality. This chapter explains how this process of expansion enables us to access deeper levels of understanding, compassion and harmony with ourselves and the world around us.

## Understanding consciousness

Consciousness can be defined as our ability to perceive, feel and understand our existence and our environment. It encompasses not only our thoughts and emotions, but also our intuition and spiritual connection. In our usual state of consciousness, we are often immersed in everyday preoccupations, repetitive thought patterns and material concerns. Expanding our consciousness means transcending these limitations to embrace a wider reality.

## Signs of expanding awareness

The process of expanding consciousness can manifest itself in many different ways. We may experience a deep sense of connection with others and with nature, an increase in intuition or a feeling of spiritual awakening. Moments of clarity, when we intuitively understand profound truths, can also occur. These experiences can be both exhilarating and unsettling, as they force us to question our habitual beliefs and perceptions.

## Practices for expanding consciousness

There are many practices we can adopt to help expand our consciousness. Meditation is one of the most powerful. By sitting in silence and concentrating on our breathing, we have the opportunity to detach ourselves from our thoughts and access a space of inner peace. This tranquility enables us to explore deeper dimensions of our being.

Mindfulness, or being present in the moment, is also an effective tool. By paying attention to our sensations, thoughts and emotions without judgment, we begin to broaden our perspective. This practice helps us to break out of automatic thought patterns and open our minds to new possibilities.

## Exploring spirituality

For many, expanding consciousness is accompanied by spiritual exploration. This can include studying and practicing spiritual philosophies, reading sacred texts or taking part in ceremonies and rituals. These practices help us connect with universal truths and understand our place in the cosmos. By immersing ourselves in spirituality, we develop a deeper sense of meaning and connection.

Spiritual journeys, whether physical or metaphysical, can also play a key role in this process. Whether through nature retreats, journeys to sacred places or deep meditation experiences, these moments can catalyze significant shifts in our consciousness.

## Openness to compassion and love

As our consciousness expands, we begin to feel greater compassion for others and ourselves. This compassion reflects our growing understanding of the interconnectedness of all things. We realize that our suffering and that of others is linked, and we develop a desire to bring Love and healing into the world.

This opening of the heart is essential if we are to live an existence aligned with our true essence. By cultivating Love and compassion, we contribute to positive change not only in our own lives, but also in the lives of others.

## The integration of expanded awareness

Expanding consciousness is not an isolated event, but an ongoing process that requires integration and practice. To reap the full benefits, it's important to bring these experiences and insights back into our daily lives. This can involve more conscious life choices, more authentic relationships, and a commitment to living in accordance with our spiritual values.

By integrating these new perspectives, we learn to navigate the world with increased wisdom, greater flexibility and deep inner peace. Expanded awareness enables us to transform challenges into opportunities for learning and growth, strengthening our resilience.

Expanding consciousness is a fascinating journey towards discovering our true nature and our place in the universe. By engaging in this process, we access an inner power that transcends the limitations of our ordinary mind. We become beings of light capable of bringing Love, compassion and understanding to a world that desperately needs them. As we realize this expansion, we awaken to a life of wholeness, harmony and connection, transforming our existence and that of those around us.

*"There is an inner strength in every human being, which once released, enables every dream, vision and desire to be transformed into reality."*

— Anthony Robbins

(Free Translation)

## OBSERVATION, AWARENESS AND TRANSMU-TATION — THE KEY TO INNER TRANSFORMATION

In our quest for inner power, three concepts are essential: observation, awareness and transmutation. These steps form a dynamic cycle that enables us not only to understand our inner world, but also to transform it. By cultivating these qualities, we can transcend our limitations and integrate our true potential.

**Observation: the foundation of self-knowledge**

Observation is the first step towards transformation. It involves paying constant, conscious attention to our thoughts, emotions and behavior without judgment. By observing ourselves, we become witnesses to our own experience. It allows us to step back and see our habitual, often automatic, patterns of thought.

Meditation is an invaluable tool for developing this capacity for observation. By sitting in silence, concentrating on our breathing and letting our thoughts pass like clouds in the sky, we learn not to identify with them. This practice helps us to see our emotional reactions and limiting beliefs with new clarity.

Observation is not limited to our inner world; it also extends to interactions with our environment. By paying attention to the signals from our surroundings, the relationships we have and the events in our lives, we can better understand what shapes our reality. Everything around us - relationships, circumstances, conflicts, etc. - tells us something about ourselves. It all acts like a mirror, reflecting where we are and what we need to work on.

### Awareness: awakening and understanding

Once we have cultivated observation, awareness emerges. This is the moment when we integrate what we've observed and begin to understand the roots of our thoughts and behaviors. This stage requires radical honesty with ourselves.

Awareness allows us to shed light on the darker areas of our psyche. We realize that our emotional reactions are not always the result of external reality, but often the reflection of our inner beliefs. For example, a fear of failure may stem from past criticism, and a tendency to self-sabotage may be rooted in a lack of self-confidence.

This understanding is liberating. It gives us the opportunity to choose how we want to respond to life's challenges, rather than reacting impulsively. By becoming aware of our patterns, we can begin to change them, opening the way to greater inner harmony.

**Transmutation: transforming the negative into the positive, in Love**

Transmutation is the final stage of this process. This is where we take the information gained through observation and awareness and use it to transform our reality. Transmutation involves an inner alchemy: transforming our fears, doubts and pain into strength, wisdom and compassion.

To transmute our negative emotions, it's crucial to welcome and re-experience them emotionally rather than rejecting them. By acknowledging our emotions, be they anger, sadness or frustration, we allow them to exist without judgment. Once accepted and re-experienced, we can release them by expressing them creatively, whether through writing, art or even movement.

The practice of gratitude also plays an important role in the transmutation process. By cultivating a sense of gratitude for the lessons learned through our challenges, we change our perspective. What was once perceived as an obstacle becomes an opportunity for growth and learning.

To conclude this chapter, observation, awareness and transmutation form a powerful cycle that guides us towards profound inner transformation. By learning to observe, become aware of and transmute our thoughts and emotions, we gradually gain access to our inner power. This process takes time and patience, but it's essential for living an authentic, fulfilling life.

By integrating these principles into our daily lives, we become not just witnesses to our own lives, but active creators of our reality. Only then can we truly embrace our unlimited potential and manifest an existence rich in meaning and light.

*"Power over others is weakness disguised as strength. Real power is inside, and it's already yours."*

— Eckhart Tolle

(Free Translation)

## ASCENSION: RAISING OUR CONSCIOUSNESS AND OUR BEING

Ascension is a concept deeply rooted in spiritual traditions the world over. It evokes the idea of an elevation of consciousness and a transformation of our being that enables us to transcend the limitations of our current existence. In the context of inner power, ascension represents a journey to a higher reality, where we can fully realize our spiritual and personal potential.

### Understanding ascension

At its core, ascension is an evolutionary process. It involves a shift in our state of consciousness, where we begin to see beyond the illusions of material reality. This process can be seen as a shift from a lower to a higher vibratory frequency, enabling us to connect to deeper levels of consciousness and truth.

This transformation is not just spiritual; it touches every aspect of our lives. By raising our consciousness, we begin to perceive our connection with everything around us. Relationships, nature and even challenges become opportunities for learning and growth. We learn to see the beauty and harmony that exist, even in difficult times.

### Stages of the climb

Ascension is a personal and unique journey for everyone. However, several stages can be identified in this process:

1. Awareness: the first step towards ascension is awareness of our current state. This involves honest introspection and the desire to grow. By recognizing our thought patterns, beliefs and behaviors, we can begin to undo what no longer serves us.

2. Release from attachments: ascension often requires the release of material and emotional attachments. This can include addictions, toxic relationships or limiting beliefs. This process of

letting go allows us to make room for new experiences and higher energy.

3. Expansion of consciousness: as we free ourselves from limitations, our consciousness begins to expand. This expansion may manifest as spiritual experiences, visions or intuitions. We begin to understand that we are much more than our physical bodies; we are beings of energy and light.

4. Alignment with our true nature: ascension invites us to align ourselves with our true essence. This means living in tune with our values, our mission and our intuition. By doing so, we attract experiences and people who resonate with our higher vibration.

5. Service and compassion: finally, ascension is also a call to serve others and express compassion. As we awaken our consciousness, we feel the need to help and inspire those around us. This selfless service strengthens our connection with humanity.

## The challenges of the climb

Although ascension is a magnificent process, it can also present challenges. Inner resistances, fears and doubts can arise at every step. We must recognize them and welcome them with compassion. As mentioned, every challenge represents an opportunity for growth and learning.

What's more, the ascension process can bring about changes in our relationships. People who no longer resonate with our new level of consciousness may move away, while others who share our vision may enter our lives. Learning to navigate these transitions gracefully is an integral part of the journey.

Ascension is an invitation to embrace our inner power and soar to new horizons. It's a journey of transformation that allows us to transcend our limitations and access a higher reality. By cultivating consciousness, releasing attachments, aligning ourselves with our true nature and serving others, we can truly experience ascension.

This process requires courage, patience and commitment to ourselves. However, it offers immeasurable rewards: a life full of meaning, connection, Love and joy. By elevating ourselves, we contribute not only to our own evolution, but also to that of humanity, the planet and even the cosmos. This is how we assume our role as beings of light in this immense universe.

*"Who looks outside, dreams; who looks inside, awakens."*

— Carl Gustav Jung

(Free Translation)

## THE CREATIVE SOURCE: THE ESSENCE OF OUR INNER POWER

In the vast panorama of spirituality, the concept of the creative source occupies a central place. It is often perceived as the origin of all existence, the universal energy that animates every living being. Understanding the creative source is fundamental to accessing our inner power and manifesting our highest potential.

### Understanding the creative source

The creative source is often described as an infinite, intangible and omnipresent force. It transcends the boundaries of religious and spiritual beliefs, manifesting itself in diverse forms across the ages and cultures. Whether called God, Universe, Primordial Energy or Consciousness, it represents the unity of all life.

This source is the matrix of creation, from which everything emerges. Every thought, emotion and action we experience comes from this fundamental energy. By recognizing our link with the source, we become aware that we are not just isolated individuals, but extensions of this creative force.

**Connecting to the source**

Connecting to the creative source is an essential part of our spiritual journey. This connection enables us to receive guidance, inspiration and creativity. It reminds us that we are co-creators of our reality, able to influence our existence through our thoughts and intentions.

To establish this connection, practices such as meditation, contemplation and prayer can be extremely beneficial. By turning inward and anchoring ourselves in the present moment, we can feel this vibrant energy surrounding us and penetrating our being. This experience of connection can manifest as moments of clarity, powerful insights or a deep sense of inner peace.

**Creativity as an expression of source**

Creativity is one of the most powerful ways in which the creative source expresses itself through us. Every creative act, whether art, music, writing or even problem-solving, is a manifestation of this divine energy. When we create, we align ourselves with the source, and our work and projects become extensions of its essence.

It's important to recognize that creativity isn't just for artists. Each of us has a unique creative potential, whether in our daily lives, our relationships or our professional projects. By cultivating our creativity, we get closer to the source and discover innovative solutions and fresh perspectives.

**The creative source and manifestation**

Understanding the creative source plays a crucial role in the manifestation process. Our thoughts and intentions, when aligned with this energy, can attract experiences and opportunities into our lives. The oft-quoted Law of Attraction is based on this connection to source.

To manifest our desires, we need to clarify

what we really want and align our emotions and feelings with our intentions. Visualization, affirmations and gratitude are tools that help us strengthen our connection to source and attract what we desire. By cultivating a positive state of mind and emitting high vibrations, we become energy magnetizers.

**The challenges of connecting to the source**

Although connecting with the creative source is an enriching experience, obstacles can arise. Doubts, fears and limiting beliefs can cloud our perception and distance us from this connection. It's crucial to approach these pitfalls with kindness and patience.

The process of deprogramming and reprogramming, already discussed in a previous chapter, is also relevant here. By working to release the beliefs that hold us back, we can open the way to a deeper connection with source. This journey takes time and practice, but the rewards are well worth it.

In short, the creative source is the very essence of our existence, an infinite reservoir of potential and creativity. By recognizing our connection with this universal energy, we access our inner power and become co-creators of our reality.

By cultivating our connection to source, expressing our creativity and aligning our intentions with our desires, we can manifest a life full of meaning and fulfillment. This journey towards understanding the creative source is an exciting adventure that invites us to explore the depths of our being and embrace our role as agents of change in the world. Ultimately, it is in this dance with source that we discover our true essence and place in the universe.

*"Spiritual awakening is the beginning of a life lived in consciousness."*

— Eckhart Tolle

(Free Translation)

## PRAYER AND MEDITATION: GATEWAYS TO INNER STRENGTH

Prayer and meditation are two spiritual practices deeply rooted in human history. Both offer powerful ways to connect with our essence, our creative source and our inner potential. Though different in their approach, these two practices share a common goal: to foster spiritual awakening and personal transformation.

### Prayer: a dialogue with the divine

Prayer can be defined as an act of communication with the divine, whether perceived as a personal entity, a universal force or consciousness. It can take many forms: requests for guidance, thanksgiving, supplication or celebration. Prayer is a way of expressing our gratitude, desires and intentions, while opening ourselves up to the wisdom and love of the source.

Prayer is not just a request, but an act of faith and trust. By praying, we acknowledge our vulnerability and need for assistance, while affirming our intention to be guided on our path. It connects us to a larger reality and reminds us that we are not alone in our struggles and triumphs.

### The different types of prayer

There are many types of prayer, each with its own purpose and intention. Among the most common are:

1. Prayer of request: this is a request for help or guidance for oneself or others. It can be directed towards specific situations or life challenges.

2. The gratitude prayer: this consists in expressing our gratitude for the blessings we have received. This practice strengthens our connection to abundance and positivity.

3. Meditative prayer: this form of prayer incorporates elements of meditation, focusing on mantras or affirmations to connect to a higher vibration.

4. Community prayer: practiced in a group, it strengthens the sense of unity and mutual support. It is often used in religious traditions to create a bond between participants.

## Meditation: an inner journey

Meditation, on the other hand, is an introspective practice designed to cultivate inner peace and mental clarity. It invites us to turn our attention inward, to calm the incessant flow of thoughts and ground ourselves in the present moment. Meditation can be a space of silence, contemplation or mindfulness, where we can explore our innermost being.

There are several meditation techniques, each offering unique benefits:

1. Mindfulness meditation: this practice involves paying attention to our thoughts, emotions and bodily sensations without judgment. It helps us develop a heightened awareness of our present experience.

2. Guided meditation: in this form, a guide or recorded voice accompanies us on a journey, often using visualizations to

help us explore our subconscious. I recommend that you choose your guide or recorded-voice meditation carefully, according to how your heart feels.

3. Mantra meditation: this technique involves repeating a sacred word or phrase to focus the mind and achieve a state of inner peace.

4. Visualization meditation: here we imagine positive images or scenarios to attract desired experiences into our lives.

**The benefits of prayer and meditation**

The benefits of prayer and meditation are many and often overlapping. Together, they contribute to our personal and spiritual development. Notable benefits include:

1. Stress reduction: both practices promote relaxation and help reduce anxiety, offering a refuge from the challenges of everyday life.

2. Mental clarity: prayer and meditation improve our concentration and our ability to make informed decisions.

3. Spiritual connection: they bring us closer to our essence and source, reinforcing our sense of belonging to something greater.

4. Emotional balance: by cultivating gratitude, compassion and inner peace, we develop greater resilience in the face of life's ups and downs.

**Integrating prayer and meditation into our lives**

To get the most out of prayer and meditation, I recommend making them part of your daily routine. Here are some practical tips:

1. Create a sacred space: create a quiet, inspiring corner of your home where you can pray and meditate without distractions.

2. Establish a routine: devote a moment each day to prayer and meditation, even if it's only a few minutes. Regularity creates powerful habits.

3. Remain open and receptive: approach these practices with an attitude of curiosity and openness. Each expe-

rience is unique and can teach you different things.

4. Combine the two: don't hesitate to mix prayer and meditation. For example, start by praying to express your intention, then move on to meditation to deepen your connection.

Prayer and meditation are effective ways of discovering our inner power. They enable us to establish a deep connection with our essence, cultivate inner peace and manifest our deepest desires. By integrating these practices into our daily lives, we can nourish our spirit, strengthen our soul and create a meaningful, fulfilling existence. This spiritual experience, imbued with devotion and contemplation, opens the door to a richer, more connected and authentic life.

*"All human beings seek the meaning of life.
The meaning of life lies in communication
with God."*

— Peter Deunov

(Free Translation)

## LANGUAGES OF LIGHT: THE EXPRESSION OF HIGHER CONSCIOUSNESS

Light languages represent a set of spiritual communications that transcend traditional words and concepts. They are often described as vibrations, symbols or energy codes that connect us to higher dimensions of consciousness. In the context of inner power and spirituality, understanding and using light languages can help us awaken our potential and amplify our connection with the universe.

### What is the language of light?

Light language is a term that encompasses various forms of spiritual communication, including symbols, sounds and frequencies that emit vibrations of love and wisdom. Unlike human languages, which are based on words and grammatical structures, light languages are non-linear and can be perceived intuitively.

These languages are often associated with experiences of meditation or communication with beings of light, spirit guides or higher entities. They are seen as a means of accessing universal wisdom and receiving teachings that nourish our spiritual evolution.

## The different forms of light language

Light languages can take many forms, each with its own characteristics and meanings:

1. Light symbols: these often appear in states of deep meditation or channeling. They may include geometric shapes, mandalas or sacred signs. Each symbol carries a unique frequency that can trigger emotional or spiritual responses in those who receive them.

2. Sounds and chants: light languages can also include sounds, mantras or chants. These sound vibrations act as catalysts to awaken higher states of consciousness. Harmonic chanting, for

example, is used to establish a connection with spiritual dimensions.

3. Light scriptures: some people receive messages or scriptures in the language of light, often in the form of texts that transcend human languages. These writings contain profound teachings and spiritual insights.

4. Visual energies: light languages can also manifest as visions or images that appear during meditation. These visions are often symbolic, and may contain personal or collective messages.

**How to access light languages**

Accessing light languages requires an open mind and a commitment to spiritual practice. Here are a few ways to get in touch with these communications:

1. Deep meditation: plunging into a meditative state can create a space conducive to the reception of light languages. By calming the mind and focusing on the breath, we can open

our consciousness to intuitive experiences.

2. Intuitive listening: practising inner listening is essential. It involves paying attention to the sensations, impressions and visions that emerge in our minds. Paying attention to these subtle messages helps us to decode the languages of light.

3. Artistic creation: art is a powerful means of expressing and receiving light languages. Whether through painting, dance or music, creative expression can channel spiritual energies, symbols and codes of light.

4. Dream work: dreams can be a gateway to the languages of light. Keeping a dream diary and analyzing the symbols and messages received can reveal profound truths and spiritual teachings.

## The benefits of light languages

Integrating the languages of light into our spiritual life can offer many advantages:

1. Spiritual awakening: these languages promote a heightened awareness of our divine essence and our connection to the universe.

2. Energy healing: symbols and light sounds (also known as light codes) can act as healing catalysts, helping to release emotional and energetic blockages.

3. Clarity and guidance: light languages often serve as a source of guidance and inspiration, providing answers to spiritual and practical questions.

4. Expanding consciousness: by working with these languages, we can expand our perception and understanding of reality, accessing higher dimensions of consciousness.

Light languages are an intense expression of our connection to the creative source and our inner potential. By opening up to these spiritual communications, we can awaken our consciousness, heal our wounds and manifest a life full of meaning and light.

This journey towards understanding the

languages of light requires patience, practice and a willingness to explore the depths of our being. By integrating these languages into our daily lives, we come closer to our true essence and our role as co-creators of our reality. Ultimately, it's in this exploration that we discover the richness of our existence and the beauty of our connection to the universe.

*"When you make peace with yourself, you make peace with the world."*

— Maha Ghosananda

(Free Translation)

# LOVE: THE UNIVERSAL FORCE OF INNER POWER

Love is one of the most powerful and transformative forces in the universe. It transcends cultural, temporal and spiritual barriers, and manifests itself in many forms. In the context of inner power and spirituality, Love is an energy, a very high vibration that connects us to our essence and that of others. Understanding and embracing this Love is crucial to raising our consciousness and realizing our spiritual potential.

## Love as creative energy

Love is often described as a creative energy, a force that animates all forms of life. It is the basis of all human interactions, relationships and experiences. This energy has the power to heal, transform and unite. When we vibrate at the frequency of Love, we align ourselves with our true nature and connect to a larger reality.

In many spiritual traditions, Love is seen as the manifestation of the creative source. It is the very essence of our existence, and by opening ourselves to this energy, we can access a depth of understanding and compassion that enriches our lives. Love is, in essence, an act of creation, enabling us to build bridges, inspire and uplift those around us.

**The different dimensions of Love**

Love manifests itself in different forms, each with its own characteristics and impact:

1. Unconditional Love: this transcends expectations and conditions. It is associated with Parental Love or Spiritual Love. In this dimension, we accept others as they are, without judgment or condition. Unconditional love is a powerful force for healing and acceptance.

2. Self-love: before we can authentically love others, we need to cultivate self-love. This means accepting, respecting and nurturing ourselves.

Self-love is the foundation on which all other forms of love are built. By honoring ourselves, we are able to offer our Love to others without reserve.

3. Brotherly love: this is the love we share with our friends, family and communities. It creates bonds and strengthens our sense of belonging. Brotherly love is a source of support and comfort, especially in difficult times.

4. Romantic love: although this type of love can be intense and passionate, it is often tinged with expectations, conflicts and desires. However, when lived in a spirit of mutual respect and understanding, romantic love can be a powerful force for unity and personal evolution.

5. Universal Love: this Love extends beyond personal boundaries and individual relationships. It is a Love that embraces all humanity and nature. Universal Love reminds us that we are all interconnected, and that every act of love, no matter how

small, has the potential to transform the world.

## Love as a tool for transformation

Love has the power to transform our lives. It pushes us to grow, evolve and transcend our limitations. In moments of pain or conflict, Love can be a healing force. By choosing to operate from Love rather than fear, we can overcome obstacles and open the way to creative solutions.

Practicing Love in our daily interactions, even in the most difficult situations, is an act of courage. It involves showing compassion, empathy and understanding, even when it seems painful. Love invites us to see beyond differences and recognize the humanity and divinity that reside in each of us.

## Cultivating love in our lives

To integrate Love into our daily lives, we can adopt several practices:

1. The practice of gratitude: recognizing and appreciating the people and experiences that nourish our hearts strengthens our connection to Love.

2. Meditation on Love: taking the time to meditate on Love, focusing on feelings of compassion and kindness, can open our hearts and expand our capacity to love.

3. Acts of kindness: engaging in acts of kindness, whether large or small, helps us to cultivate Love in our daily lives. These gestures create waves of positive energy that touch not only those who receive them, but ourselves too.

4. Active listening: practicing active listening and offering our attention to others is a powerful way of transmitting Love. It strengthens bonds and makes others feel valued and understood.

Love is a powerful, transformative force that forms the basis of our inner power. By expressing Love in all its forms, we can enrich not only our own lives, but also the lives of those around us.

The practice of Love, whether unconditional, fraternal or universal, connects us to our essence and reminds us of our role as co-creators of reality. By choosing to live in Love, we open the door to an existence full of meaning, connection and spiritual fulfillment. Love, as a universal vibration, is the key to accessing our inner power and realizing our highest potential.

*"We're here to save a planet: so this is no ordinary existence, in which we assume only a modest role. We've come here to embody our magnificence, which means embracing the noble prowess of what we're ready to heal and rehabilitate internally, thus giving the whole of humanity an example of what's possible in this movement of the divine feminine Christ."*

— Kaia Ra

(Free Translation)

# UNITY: THE DEEP CONNECTION OF ALL LIFE

Unity is a fundamental concept in spirituality, often described as the recognition of our intrinsic connection to all that exists. In a world where diversity is celebrated, unity reminds us that, despite our differences, we are all part of the same web of life. Understanding and integrating this principle of unity is primordial to accessing our inner power and living a meaningful existence.

## The nature of the unit

Unity transcends physical, cultural and mental boundaries. It invites us to see beyond the superficial appearances and distinctions that separate us. This holistic vision teaches us that every human being, every element of nature, even every thought and emotion, is interconnected.

In many spiritual traditions, unity is seen as a manifestation of the creative source, the primordial energy that animates all existence. By recognizing this interconnectedness, we can begin to understand our place in the universe and our role in the grand scheme of life.

**The benefits of unity awareness**

Here are the benefits:

1. Reducing separation: awareness of our unity with others helps us transcend feelings of separation and isolation. This awareness fosters deeper, more authentic relationships based on understanding and compassion.

2. Empathy and compassion: by realizing that each of us feels pain, joy and struggle, we develop a natural empathy for others. This compassion strengthens our common humanity and motivates us to act for the well-being of others.

3. Harmony with nature: unity also teaches us to respect and cherish nature. By recognizing that we are part of this ecosystem, we are

motivated to protect our environment and live in harmony with it.

4. Spiritual awakening: understanding unity opens us up to profound spiritual experiences. It enables us to transcend our ego and connect with higher levels of consciousness, furthering our spiritual evolution.

**The challenges of unity**

Although unity is a powerful principle, there can be challenges to its integration. Fears, prejudices and limiting beliefs can create barriers that prevent us from feeling this connection. So it's vital to work on these obstacles by engaging in a process of deprogramming and reprogramming, as discussed earlier in this book.

What's more, living in unity in a world that often values separation and individualism can be difficult. However, every small step towards harmony and understanding counts. By deliberately choosing to cultivate unity, we help to create positive change, not only within ourselves, but also in the world around us.

Unity is a fundamental truth that connects us

all, transcending superficial differences and reminding us of our common essence. By integrating this principle into our daily lives, we develop a deeper awareness of our place in the universe and our role as co-creators of reality.

Unity invites us to love diversity while recognizing that every individual, every element of nature, and every thought are manifestations of the same source. It is in this understanding that we find our true inner power. By living in unity, we create a more loving, compassionate and harmonious world, for ourselves and for future generations.

*"Pray, meditate and ask for help. It will be given to you if you persevere."*

— La Porte-Parole Anonymous

Reception and transcription of the Letters and Articles dictated by Christ

(Free Translation)

# GALACTICS: MESSENGERS OF UNIVERSAL CONS-CIOUSNESS

The universe is vast and mysterious, and our place within it is often a source of questioning. Galactic beings, perceived as entities from other worlds or dimensions, occupy a fascinating place in contemporary spirituality. They are seen as messengers of universal consciousness, bringing teachings, energies and perspectives that can enrich our understanding of ourselves and our role in the universe.

## Who are the galactics?

Those who have been contacted by galactics, or who have contacted them, describe them as beings of energy and light from different planets, solar systems or dimensions. They can include races such as the Pleiadians, Arcturians, Végalians, Sirians and many others, each carrying their own set of teachings and vibrations and frequencies.

These beings are often described as having a high level of consciousness ($5^e$ dimension and above: highly evolved beings) and a deep understanding of universal laws. They are considered guardians of spiritual wisdom and guides for humanity, aiming to help us evolve towards higher states of consciousness.

However, discernment is required, as galactics below the $5^e$ dimension are rather involutive, like reptilians and others. Contact with these beings should be avoided.

To discern, let's rely on what our intuition and heart feel and what emanates from them (love, kindness - how do we feel in their presence?). Let's ask them to identify themselves (who are they and where do they come from?) and then act accordingly.

### The galactic connection

Establishing a connection with the galactics may seem mysterious, but there are many spiritual practices that help us open up to their presence.

Here are a few ways to cultivate this connection:

1. Meditation and astral travel: meditation is a powerful tool for accessing higher dimensions of consciousness, as we have already seen. By meditating, we can create the right space to receive messages or energies from the galactics. Some practitioners report experiences of astral travel, where they feel transported to other worlds and encounter galactic beings.

2. Intuition and inner listening: listening to our intuition and feelings is essential for establishing a link with these entities. Messages from the galactics can manifest as intuitions, inner visions, im-pressions or tele-pathic communications through thought or heart-to-heart.

3. Symbols and light languages: galactics often use symbols and light languages (light codes) to convey their messa-ges. Meditations centered on these symbols can open channels of communication with them.

4. Rituals and ceremonies: creating rituals to honor galactic energies can strengthen our connection. This can include using crystals, incense and chanting to attract their presence and receive their guidance.

**The teachings of the galactics**

The galactics bring a multitude of teachings that can enrich our spiritual journey:

1. Unity and interconnection: one of the most powerful messages from the galactics is that of unity. They remind us that we are all part of a whole, that our personal evolution is intrinsically linked to that of the whole of humanity, the planet and even the universe.

2. Love and compassion: galactics embody vibrations of unconditional love and compassion. They encourage us to cultivate these qualities in our daily interactions and to transform ourselves through Love.

3. Spiritual evolution: they teach us that spiritual evolution is a continuous

process. By opening ourselves up to new ideas and experiences, we can transcend our limitations and reach higher levels of consciousness.

4. Spiritual technology: galactics have an advanced understanding of technology, not only on the material plane, but also on the spiritual. They encourage us to explore technologies that support our awakening, including meditation practices, energy healing, intuitive communication, activations, density dismantling and more.

## The challenges of the galactic connection

While connecting with galactics can be rewarding, it can also present challenges. Fear of the unknown, doubts and limiting beliefs can create obstacles. It's crucial to approach this journey with open-mindedness and discernment, remaining grounded in our earthly reality while exploring these higher dimensions.

In addition, it's important to remember that each individual has his or her own experience with galactics. What works for one may not resonate for another. We need to be attentive to our own feelings and respect our personal pace in this exploration.

Galactics represent a fascinating facet of our quest for inner power and spiritual awakening. By establishing a connection with these beings of light, we can access profound teachings that enrich our understanding of ourselves and our place in the universe.

By integrating and embodying their messages of unity, Love and evolution, we can transform our reality and contribute to positive change in the world. This adventure into galactic connection reminds us that we're not alone on our path, and that the universe is filled with wisdom and energies ready to guide us to our highest potential. Ultimately, this exploration brings us closer to our divine essence and our role as co-creators of reality.

# EPILOGUE

As we come to the end of this journey through "Activate your inner power for a new life", it's appropriate to take a moment to reflect on all we've explored together. Each chapter has been designed not only to inform you, but above all to inspire you to take action, to dive deep within yourself and unleash the power within.

Throughout these pages, you've discovered strategies for overcoming the obstacles that can stand in your way. You've learned that connecting to your inner power lies not in grandiose feats, but in the small, everyday actions that nourish your mind and soul. It's in moments of stillness, reflection and introspection that true transformation begins.

As you integrate these lessons into your life, remember that the path to a fulfilled existence is an ongoing journey. Every step you take towards authenticity, self-confidence and passion is a step towards a new life. It's normal to encounter challenges along the way, but every obstacle is an opportunity to grow, learn and strengthen that connection with your true, divine essence.

As you close this book soon, take with you the teachings and reflections that have resonated with you. Commit to continuing this exploration, nurturing your inner power and living each day with intention. By sharing your light, Love and energy with the world, you become a catalyst for change, not only for yourself, but also for those around you and indeed, for all humanity and the cosmos.

Your journey doesn't end here. It's just beginning. Dare to dream big, dare to connect to your power and create the life that calls to you. Remember that you are the creator of your reality, and every day is a new opportunity to write your story. Move forward with courage and passion, because the best is yet to come.

# MY STORY

I'm Lisa Collins. I'll try to be brief, as I have so many wonderful things to say.

I had a happy childhood and adolescence. At the age of 18, I left my hometown and moved to Montreal to study, and later, to work. For me, it was a time of discovery and fulfillment. After a few years, I explored married life. From the age of 29 onwards, my experiences of relationships with spouses were very difficult. I searched tirelessly for the light through it all, but I wasn't listening to my heart...

As a teenager, I became interested in personal growth and spirituality. I read a lot. Then in 2011, when I read Wayne W. Dyer's "The Power of

Intention", I decided to start meditating for twenty minutes a day. After a while, I noticed the benefits of these meditations: peace and inner calm. I continued to meditate and still do today.

From 2017 to 2022, I undertook various workshops and training courses in meditation and in channeling very high frequencies from highly evolved galactics (Pleiadians, Arcturians, Sirians and others) with two transmitters, one French and the second German. With them, I learned to connect with these beings of light, to channel their high frequencies and to receive activations, purifications, resets, energetic healing, etc.

During these years, my inner transformation began and my life also changed, drastically, in all areas, in order to live other experiences. I received a lot of light and information, which, depending on my path and what I was ready to let go of, forced the negative to rise up and be transmuted. All this learning was intensive and I needed time to integrate it all. My inner vision and feelings developed over the years.

And in 2018, I've started a training with a group of evolved Vegalian beings. The training lasted a few years, and then our common mission began in earnest.

It was a revelation for me.

With them, I help our humanity to awaken, to raise their frequencies and develop their consciousness to access higher planes, while embodying their divinity in their daily activities and relationships, here and now.

I'm very grateful to these beings for everything they've enabled me to experience and become since I've been in contact with them. They have given meaning to my life. I've finally found what I've always been looking for.

My special thanks go to Ismaya, from my heart to his, for his unconditional love, his devotion, his understanding and for all the support and care he has given me along the way.

****

# SUGGESTED READINGS

AIRD, Kishori, *L'ADN démystifié: Guide pratique de reprogrammation des treize hélices au point zéro*, Tome 1, Institut Kishori Inc., Nouvelle édition, 2007.

BAILEY, Alice A., 3 volumes: *Initiation, human & solar; The consciousness of the atom; Letters on occult meditation*, Premium Classic Books, 2018.

BEAUREGARD, Mario et O'LEARY, Denise, *Du cerveau à Dieu: Plaidoyer d'un neuroscientifique pour l'existence de l'âme*, Guy Trédaniel, 2015.

BERNARD, Patrick, *Le Pouvoir Miraculeux de la Conscience, Carnet de pèlerinage intérieur*, Les Éditions Déni Communications Inc., 2012.

BRADEN, Gregg, *The divine matrix: bringing time, space, miracles and belief*, Hay House LLC, 2008.

BRADEN, Gregg, *Wisdom Codes: ancient words to rewire our brains and heal our hearts*, Hay House LLC,

2021.

BRENNAN, Barbara Ann, *Guérir par la lumière*, coll. « Le corps à vivre », Tchou, 1993.

BROWN, Michael, *Le processus de la Présence, Un voyage dans la conscience du moment présent*, Ariane Éditions Inc., 2012.

DEBAKER, Laurent, *Ho'oponopono: Le pouvoir en vous*, Audio Book, ADA audio, 2017.

DEUNOV, Peter, *Le Livre de la Prière: Tout est possible pour celui qui s'ouvre à l'énergie de la prière*, Éditions Ultima, 2009.

DISPENZA, Joe, *You are the placebo: making your mind matter*, Hay House LLC, 2015.

DISPENZA, Joe, *Breaking the habit of being yourself: How to lose your mind and create a new one*, Generic, 2013.

EDEN, Donna et FEINSTEIN, David, *Médecine énergétique: éveiller le guérisseur en vous*, Ariane, 2005.

FERRINI, Paul, *L'amour sans conditions: Réflexions de l'Esprit Christique*, Le Dauphin Blanc, 2006.

FINLEY, Guy, *The secret of letting go*, Llewellyn Publications, 2007.

FINLEY, Guy, *Soyez votre propre lumière, Éclairez votre cœur, votre âme et votre esprit*, Les Éditions de l'Homme, 2008.

SCHUCMAN, Helen, *A course in miracles*, Foundation for inner peace, 2007.

KABAT-ZINN, Dr. Jon, *Au cœur de la tourmente, la pleine conscience: Le manuel complet de MBSR, ou réduction du stress basée sur la mindfulness*, J'ai lu – Bien-être, 2009.

KHAN, Kashif et THORN, Rod, *The DNA way: Unlock the secrets of your genes to reverse disease, slow aging, and achieve optimal wellness*, Hay House, Inc., 2023.

LA PORTE-PAROLE – Anonyme, *Les lettres du Christ: Le Christ est revenu*, Interkeltia-Atlantes, 2012.

NALLET, Françoise, *Mémoires cellulaires: Les clés de votre réalité intérieure*, Guy Trédaniel éditeur, 2023.

OUELLET, Francine et DELADURANTAYE, André, *Mon retour par l'intégration christique avec « Lumière de l'Être » - Énergie Christique*, Les Éditions Marie-Lakshmi, 2000.

Propos recueillis par VALLÉE, Martine, *Le grand potentiel humain – Les Pléiadiens, les Hathors et les Arcturiens: Marcher dans la lumière*, Ariane, 2013.

RA, Kaia, *The Sophia Code: A living transmission from the Sophia dragon tribe*, Kaia Ra and Ra-El Publishing, 2016.

RINPOCHÉ, Sogyal, *Le livre tibétain de la vie et de la mort*, Nouvelle édition augmentée, La Table Ronde, 2003.

TOLLE, Eckhart, *Le pouvoir du moment présent, Guide d'éveil spirituel*, Ariane Éditions Inc., 2000.

9 782924 818831